Developing Managers for Business Performance

What your board needs to know today

First published 2002
Reprinted 2002, 2004

Cover design by Curve
Designed and typeset by Beacon GDT
Printed in Great Britain by Short Run Press

British Library Cataloguing in Publication Data
A catalogue record for this book is available from the British Library

ISBN 0 85292 960 9

Chartered Institute of Personnel and Development,
CIPD House, Camp Road, London SW19 4UX

Tel: 020 8971 9000
Fax: 020 8263 3333
Website: www.cipd.co.uk

Incorporated by Royal Charter. Registered charity no. 1079797.

Contents

Acknowledgements

The CIPD would like to thank the project team:

- Simon Court for leading the CIPD research team. Simon is managing director of Value Partnership Ltd, a consultancy that works with clients to implement strategies that create value. Previous roles include director of two major companies and a background in management development.

- Don Young, chairman of Value Partnership Ltd. Don has held senior executive roles for global companies in marketing, operations, and organisation and HR management. He has been a director of two British Plcs.

- Charlotte Chambers, Value Partnership Ltd. Charlotte was dean of management at a leading business school and served as director for management development responsible for the development of managers worldwide for a major plc.

And for her contribution to the earlier work:

- Dr Jenny Quantrell. Jenny works as strategic adviser to boards, top teams and change agents.

The Institute would also like to acknowledge all those senior executives who participated in the research and contributed to the development of the executive briefing. In particular, members of the advisory group for the project and senior executives at Shell, Christ's Hospital Foundation, the Civil Service College, and Consignia.

The project was managed on behalf of the Institute by Karen Giles, Adviser, Organisation and Development at the CIPD.

Foreword

Increasingly today, we can see two quite distinct streams of top management behaviour. One might be characterised as the 'transactional' school, where the main emphasis is on the trading and exploitation of assets and the squeezing of organisational costs to the bone. The second stream is characterised by a focus on the business process and on developing an organisation that is capable of performing better than its competitors.

Some very successful organisations combine something of both streams, skilfully blending a focus on the quality of organisation and management with, for example, making and assimilating strategic acquisitions. On the other hand, there are enough contemporary examples to fill several books of corporate disaster caused by attempting to grow by the transactional route without creating a superior organisation.

This Executive Briefing is about making linkages between management development and business performance. The research that underpins the briefing identified some very good examples of organisations that are establishing successful ways of improving performance and planning for the future of the business, by integrating a review of the quality of organisation and management into the planning process.

However, it is also clear that many organisations have not yet succeeded in establishing effective linkages between the business, organisation and the requirements of management. In these cases, it is evident that the development of management capability has been marginalised from the business, and senior executives have not yet acknowledged or addressed the challenges involved.

This briefing is intended to be of practical assistance to those who wish to enhance their strategic contribution to the future performance of their organisations.

Don Beattie

President
Chartered Institute of Personnel and Development

Executive summary

Drawing on new and extensive CIPD research, this briefing focuses on the connection between corporate performance and business, organisation and management development strategies. It is primarily addressed to senior executives in UK organisations who are seeking to review the quality of their management development strategy and improve its contribution to the business.

This briefing sets in context the nature of the management challenge in the UK and then, pulling together the voices and experiences of senior executives themselves, offers a practical framework for strengthening the links between business challenges and management development interventions.

At the core of the competitive challenge is a recognition that:

◘ *'Businesses are {primarily} people constrained, not £ constrained' (Senior manager, Shell International Ltd)*

Increasingly, senior management knows that the ability to identify, manage and retain talent is critical to sustaining business performance. It realises that the breadth and depth of management capability is key to creating organisations capable of continuously anticipating change and exploiting opportunities for growth. Even the investment community is starting to challenge companies about the quality of their management competence, beyond the chief executive and top team.

Yet CIPD research shows that many organisations are putting their performance at risk because management development itself continues to be a victim of poor management practice, disconnected from the business imperatives and challenges of the enterprise.

It is therefore not surprising in the context of this research that:

◘ *senior managers see the biggest challenge for their organisations as 'integrating management development with the implementation of organisational goals'.*

Respondents from over 400 organisations in the UK and Ireland to a CIPD survey revealed this was the key priority for their organisations (86 per cent). How do senior managers make sense of the management contribution to business performance? What are the key processes and relationships involved? And how can those accountable for leading development build a shared responsibility with senior colleagues for developing managers?

Through the knowledge, practice and experience of senior executives and experts the briefing identifies:

◘ *three key and mutually reinforcing* **requirements** *for connecting business challenges and management development:*

1 Making the case for developing managers: convincing key stakeholders of the significance of management to business performance

2 Making the connection between business strategies, organisation and management development: clarifying the business purpose and outcomes for investing in management

3 Managing the learning – getting the implementation right: designing, specifying, implementing and evaluating management development strategies that are 'fit for purpose'.

The framework recognises that senior managers make choices about the significance of management to business performance and that the nature of management roles varies between organisations. It focuses on 'how to' deliver a business-focused management development response appropriate to specific organisational contexts and constraints.

Requirement 1

- *Making the case means clarifying twin purposes for developing managers – to deliver the current business model and to develop future business models. Each purpose requires its own distinctive approaches and each needs to be adapted and customised to the people and the organisation it exists to serve.*

Both purposes are clearly important, and a few leading organisations in the UK are increasingly focusing on managing the two purposes as a coherent approach.

What are the implications for the nature of the development task, the way to organise to deliver development, the approach to evaluation and the learning vehicles that are used?

Requirement 2

- *Connecting business strategies with organisation and management requirements relies on effective strategic management and Business, Organisation and Management Review (BOMR) processes.*

Two features distinguish organisations that are seeking to forge effective linkages between business challenges and the development of managers. First, they have a robust strategic management process that makes organisational and management needs explicit, and integrates these into the business plan. Second, there is rigorous dialogue among senior managers across the business, within a framework to review, continuously, how managers are expected to deliver business success (BOMR).

Survey evidence shows that many organisations in the UK have yet to establish these processes effectively. So how do you lead the development of a BOMR process in your organisation? What are the key characteristics, and what might the content and outcomes of a review process look like?

Building on case study material from a range of organisations in the UK, the briefing shares examples of how others are integrating management development with business plans and outlines a process framework for engaging colleagues in getting started.

Requirement 3

- *Managing the learning: however good your management development action, value is created or destroyed by how well you make the case and make the connection, so managing learning well is not enough.*

Implementation issues include diagnosing, specifying, implementing and evaluating the contribution of management development to organisational performance.

The research discovered some imaginative management development initiatives, but in most cases these arose from a link with business performance.

This briefing emphasises the ongoing need to ensure that management development is geared around contributing to sustained business performance – by being reviewed within the BOMR, and organised and managed to deliver on the twin business purposes outlined above.

The briefing explores some key challenges and practices in implementing management development for business outcomes. In particular, it looks at emerging thinking in leading companies on how to measure the impact of their management development investment on the business.

◘ *Are you confident that your organisation is developing managers who are fit for the current and future challenges of your business?*

If you want to take further positive action to develop your organisation's management capability as a platform for sustained business performance, the briefing offers a checklist to assess performance and prioritise action.

The first chapter outlines:

◩ **the business context of the contribution of managers to the UK corporate performance challenge**

◩ **senior executives' views of the critical issues in developing managers**

◩ **key terms in the executive briefing.**

Executive summary

Drawing on new and extensive CIPD research, this briefing focuses on the connection between corporate performance and business, organisation and management development strategies. It is primarily addressed to senior executives in UK organisations who are seeking to review the quality of their management development strategy and improve its contribution to the business.

This briefing sets in context the nature of the management challenge in the UK and then, pulling together the voices and experiences of senior executives themselves, offers a practical framework for strengthening the links between business challenges and management development interventions.

At the core of the competitive challenge is a recognition that:

◨ *'Businesses are {primarily} people constrained, not £ constrained' (Senior manager, Shell International Ltd)*

Increasingly, senior management knows that the ability to identify, manage and retain talent is critical to sustaining business performance. It realises that the breadth and depth of management capability is key to creating organisations capable of continuously anticipating change and exploiting opportunities for growth. Even the investment community is starting to challenge companies about the quality of their management competence, beyond the chief executive and top team.

Yet CIPD research shows that many organisations are putting their performance at risk because management development itself continues to be a victim of poor management practice, disconnected from the business imperatives and challenges of the enterprise.

It is therefore not surprising in the context of this research that:

◨ *senior managers see the biggest challenge for their organisations as 'integrating management development with the implementation of organisational goals'.*

Respondents from over 400 organisations in the UK and Ireland to a CIPD survey revealed this was the key priority for their organisations (86 per cent). How do senior managers make sense of the management contribution to business performance? What are the key processes and relationships involved? And how can those accountable for leading development build a shared responsibility with senior colleagues for developing managers?

Through the knowledge, practice and experience of senior executives and experts the briefing identifies:

- *three key and mutually reinforcing **requirements** for connecting business challenges and management development:*

1 Making the case for developing managers: convincing key stakeholders of the significance of management to business performance

2 Making the connection between business strategies, organisation and management development: clarifying the business purpose and outcomes for investing in management

3 Managing the learning – getting the implementation right: designing, specifying, implementing and evaluating management development strategies that are 'fit for purpose'.

The framework recognises that senior managers make choices about the significance of management to business performance and that the nature of management roles varies between organisations. It focuses on 'how to' deliver a business-focused management development response appropriate to specific organisational contexts and constraints.

Requirement 1

- *Making the case means clarifying twin purposes for developing managers – to deliver the current business model and to develop future business models. Each purpose requires its own distinctive approaches and each needs to be adapted and customised to the people and the organisation it exists to serve.*

Both purposes are clearly important, and a few leading organisations in the UK are increasingly focusing on managing the two purposes as a coherent approach.

What are the implications for the nature of the development task, the way to organise to deliver development, the approach to evaluation and the learning vehicles that are used?

Requirement 2

- *Connecting business strategies with organisation and management requirements relies on effective strategic management and Business, Organisation and Management Review (BOMR) processes.*

Two features distinguish organisations that are seeking to forge effective linkages between business challenges and the development of managers. First, they have a robust strategic management process that makes organisational and management needs explicit, and integrates these into the business plan. Second, there is rigorous dialogue among senior managers across the business, within a framework to review, continuously, how managers are expected to deliver business success (BOMR).

Foreword

Increasingly today, we can see two quite distinct streams of top management behaviour. One might be characterised as the 'transactional' school, where the main emphasis is on the trading and exploitation of assets and the squeezing of organisational costs to the bone. The second stream is characterised by a focus on the business process and on developing an organisation that is capable of performing better than its competitors.

Some very successful organisations combine something of both streams, skilfully blending a focus on the quality of organisation and management with, for example, making and assimilating strategic acquisitions. On the other hand, there are enough contemporary examples to fill several books of corporate disaster caused by attempting to grow by the transactional route without creating a superior organisation.

This Executive Briefing is about making linkages between management development and business performance. The research that underpins the briefing identified some very good examples of organisations that are establishing successful ways of improving performance and planning for the future of the business, by integrating a review of the quality of organisation and management into the planning process.

However, it is also clear that many organisations have not yet succeeded in establishing effective linkages between the business, organisation and the requirements of management. In these cases, it is evident that the development of management capability has been marginalised from the business, and senior executives have not yet acknowledged or addressed the challenges involved.

This briefing is intended to be of practical assistance to those who wish to enhance their strategic contribution to the future performance of their organisations.

Don Beattie

President
Chartered Institute of Personnel and Development

Contents

Acknowledgements

The CIPD would like to thank the project team:

- Simon Court for leading the CIPD research team. Simon is managing director of Value Partnership Ltd, a consultancy that works with clients to implement strategies that create value. Previous roles include director of two major companies and a background in management development.

- Don Young, chairman of Value Partnership Ltd. Don has held senior executive roles for global companies in marketing, operations, and organisation and HR management. He has been a director of two British Plcs.

- Charlotte Chambers, Value Partnership Ltd. Charlotte was dean of management at a leading business school and served as director for management development responsible for the development of managers worldwide for a major plc.

And for her contribution to the earlier work:

- Dr Jenny Quantrell. Jenny works as strategic adviser to boards, top teams and change agents.

The Institute would also like to acknowledge all those senior executives who participated in the research and contributed to the development of the executive briefing. In particular, members of the advisory group for the project and senior executives at Shell, Christ's Hospital Foundation, the Civil Service College, and Consignia.

The project was managed on behalf of the Institute by Karen Giles, Adviser, Organisation and Development at the CIPD.

Developing Managers for Business Performance

What your board needs to know today

First published 2002
Reprinted 2002, 2004

Cover design by Curve
Designed and typeset by Beacon GDT
Printed in Great Britain by Short Run Press

British Library Cataloguing in Publication Data
A catalogue record for this book is available from the British Library

ISBN 0 85292 960 9

Chartered Institute of Personnel and Development,
CIPD House, Camp Road, London SW19 4UX

Tel: 020 8971 9000
Fax: 020 8263 3333
Website: www.cipd.co.uk

Incorporated by Royal Charter. Registered charity no. 1079797.

Developing Managers for Business Performance

The Chartered Institute of Personnel and Development is the leading publisher of books and reports for personnel and training professionals, students, and all those concerned with the effective management and development of people at work. For full details of all our titles, please contact the Publishing Department:

Tel: 020 8263 3387
Fax: 020 8263 3850

E-mail: publish@cipd.co.uk

The catalogue of all CIPD titles can be viewed on the CIPD website:
www.cipd.co.uk/publications

Overcoming the blockages to making the case within an organisation

Some of the management cultures that exist in our organisations are a considerable obstacle to making the case for developing managers. We need to understand what the current range of attitudes and behaviours towards management are. Here are some that we have observed:

◘ Management is only about *top management*. Venture capitalists often hold this view. They are not alone, as many chief executives think like this – even some at business schools.

◘ Management is a *battleground*. In some firms management is effectively a constant series of battles over turf, resources, ideology, or whatever.

◘ Management is *overlooked* as an issue. It just is not seen in many corporate contexts. The focus is all on analysis and business decisions. Conventional MBA programmes attempt to teach business, not management.

◘ Management is *doing things*. Planning, co-ordinating, controlling, and so on. You just need to learn 'how to'. Look at the 'menu' of training programmes offered by many HR and training functions.

> *'Some of the management cultures that exist in our organisations are a considerable obstacle to making the case for developing managers.*

◘ The *living company* view of management. We have borrowed the expression of Arie de Geus (*The Living Company: Growth, Learning and Longevity in Business*, 1999) to capture the adaptive characteristics of this view. A handful of leading companies are evolving models of organisation and management that will enable them to challenge existing markets, innovate and create future markets.

These are just some of a range of views about management and the value impact of management. Notice that only the 'living company' view is rooted in an understanding of the variety of ways in which the actions and decisions of managers throughout an organisation add or destroy value.

The challenge for the HR director is to understand the attitudes in their own organisation and to turn obstacles into 'hooks' that help to make the case. For example, by using successes at top level to justify making broader investments in developing managers.

In organisations that predominantly employ autonomous professionals, such as research scientists, investment bankers, television programme makers, teachers and lawyers, 'management' is an activity that has often emerged later in people's careers, and the early focus of people's training has been only on professional competence. Getting people to give attention to and develop skills in an activity that is, in many cases, regarded as low level and administrative is difficult. It must be handled in a highly individual way, in the first instance by addressing issues on a 'just-in-time' basis, until the professional has understood more completely what 'management' or 'leadership' is all about.

In order to intervene, two key issues must be grasped by whoever is responsible for leading development:

1   The rational argument for investing, based on a thorough understanding of the business; and

2   The impact of the management culture and politics and how to get sufficient leverage to make change happen.

Neither is sufficient alone. But most of all we need to take responsibility for the problem. In the course of this study, one senior HR person with whom we talked described the tremendous competitive pressure on their organisation and the imperative to change a bureaucratic and hierarchical structure and culture, and then laid out the range of actions being pursued. When asked if these actions would be enough to achieve the change required in the timescales available, the answer was 'No, but it's the best I can do'. How would you feel about this response if you had a stake in this organisation?

Use this chapter to explore:

- **how effective your organisation is at connecting strategy and management development**

- **how a Business, Organisation and Management Review (BOMR) process can improve business-focused management development and**

- **how you can take the lead.**

3 | Making the connection between business strategy, organisation and management development

Many management teams have failed to make the link between business plans, organisation and management development. This briefing presents a challenge to HR directors to take full responsibility for making this link within their own organisation, so that it can respond to the increasingly competitive challenges of the future. In our survey we found that only 16 per cent of our senior management respondents believed they were 'very effective' at developing business plans that specify the management capabilities required. Anecdotal evidence supports this: one leading business school told us that HR director clients often cannot say what they are trying to achieve in business terms from programmes to develop managers.

Where an organisation obtains least impact from developing its managers, people do not see any connection between the job they do and the overall performance of the organisation. As a result, they cannot see any great connection between organisational effectiveness and the development that they undertake.

During this project, we found organisations where the senior management team had little understanding of, or apparent interest in, the connection between people's capability and commitment, the creation of value and business performance. They were heavily driven by deal making or acquisitions, or focusing only on costs and short-term measures, or so taken up with intellectual or hierarchical élitism that they had overlooked the imperative to create value for customers.

What can we learn from these observations? The quality of the connection between the business strategy, organisation and management depends on the quality of the strategic management process in an organisation. This quality depends on factors such as:

◘ good-quality information

◘ broad stakeholder involvement

◘ rigorous analysis

◘ robust debate

◘ clear, focused success criteria.

This gives us three potential scenarios. Which one is yours?

Scenario 1

- Strategic management process provides model for creating value

- Organisation and management specified in the model

This is the place to be: a business model and strategy that makes explicit the connection between the development of managers and business success.

Scenario 2

- Strategic management process provides a financial and market-focused model for creating value

- Organisation and management are not integrated into the model

The business model is all externally focused in this scenario, and senior managers have 'overlooked' organisation and management development. The challenge here is to broaden the business model to clarify how managers are expected to deliver business success. This means a role for some kind of Business, Organisation and Management Review (BOMR) process (see page 19).

Scenario 3

- Strategic management process provides only financial performance targets

- Organisation and management are not seen as business objectives

This scenario is a common problem. In such a setting, the senior HR person has to begin to make the links based on the business case discussed in the previous section. This involves making clear the assumptions that are implied by business targets (eg managers who are capable of innovating when this is not the track record) and creating opportunities for people to test these assumptions. If competitive pressures or environmental forces are powerful, the HR person may be in a stronger position to get the attention of others in the top team by demonstrating the immediate and longer-term impact of failing to use development and other people processes for the benefit of the organisation. Asking good questions and opening your argument up to scrutiny will begin to influence the agenda positively. We met excellent examples of our respondents doing just that, sometimes by stealth and sometimes more openly.

Overall, the capability to make the connection between the development of the business, the organisation and managers is extremely variable. This variation can partly be attributed to different business contexts and the very different economic resources that can be invested in learning and development. But a much more significant factor seems to be the extent to which both senior line managers and the person with HR responsibility understand and engage in fruitful dialogue about those fundamental connections between business models and management's capability to deliver them.

Learning to make the connections between success and capability – the BOMR

The Business, Organisation and Management Review (BOMR) process aims to develop the understanding of senior people about the organisation and management preconditions for business success and to help them to use these insights to plan for change. This involves, first and foremost, making clear the assumptions that are built into the business plan and creating opportunities for people to test out these assumptions. It should be part of the strategic management process of a company. An effective BOMR is tailored to the situation and context of the business. It is also designed for the people who will be expected to participate in it. For example, if there are strong linkages between business units, the BOMR process should be designed in such a way that those linkages are fully explored.

The key output from the perspective of developing management capability is a clear view of the contribution expected from managers to today's

and tomorrow's business models, and a business-centred brief for managers and developers to work from.

> **'The Business, Organisation and Management Review (BOMR) process aims to develop the understanding of senior people about the organisation and management preconditions for business success and to help them to use these insights to plan for change'**

Leading the organisation and management review for your business

So, how do you lead the development of a BOMR process in your business? An effective BOMR process would have a number of characteristics:

- ◘ An emphasis on quality of dialogue rather than on the mechanics of the process, with a minimum of paperwork and bureaucracy. It should be exploratory and relatively 'loose', as the aim is to cause managers to think laterally about factors that often cannot be directly connected.

- ◘ Is likely to be 'bottom-up' – that is, initiated at the business unit rather than corporate level – but to a framework of questioning and thinking that may be corporately provided.

- ◘ Will be forward looking, anticipating short- or medium-term business threats and opportunities and the capabilities these might test and require.

◘ Needs an appropriate balance in its focus between sustaining the current business model and developing future business models. Both are important, and the relative balance between the two will change dynamically over time.

◘ Works best when repeated over several cycles, as practice, dialogue and learning seem to enable managers to see more and more connections between performance and organisation. Involvement becomes a developmental experience for the senior management group.

◘ CEO sponsorship of the process and a clear specification of the other roles are required if the process is to be a success.

◘ Not allowing politics and personalities to cloud the real issues, eg the value of certain linkages between businesses.

Before getting into the BOMR itself, a word about preparation. Information will need to be collected (see the checklist on page 31) and people briefed on how to get the most value from the process. The whole process demands facilitation with a clear focus on the outcomes required for the business, an obvious role for the most senior HR person or the person with the strongest capabilities in this area.

What might the content of a review process look like?

Business, Organisation and Management Review – outline

1 Overall aims of the review process

To encourage managers, especially general managers, to explore:

◘ The connections between the business model(s) that will enable the enterprise to succeed in its competitive environment and the distinctive competencies that will support them.

◘ The gap between performance goals and actual performance and the required characteristics and capabilities of the organisation.

2 Content of the BOMR process

Overall, this can be broken down into two parts:

Part One aims to help managers think about the relationships between the business of the enterprise and its organisation. The output is likely to be a series of actions that will affect strategy, operations, organisation and people (not just organisation and people).

Part Two will focus more directly on the range of HR actions, programmes and processes that will be needed to support the effective functioning of the particular enterprise. This would include activities to develop managers.

Part One – typical content

Review and discussion of:

◩ the challenges facing the business in its competitive markets

◩ the key strategies that will enable the enterprise to succeed, and the specific targets and goals for the planning period

◩ the current and future business model(s) for the particular business, and the organisational and management capabilities that will enable the business to deliver the strategies/respond to the challenges

◩ the actual performance of the business, and any major performance shortfalls/gaps

◩ the organisation and how well it is working, including a review of business and management processes, roles, responsibilities and relationships.

From the definitions of the strategies, performance goals and the actual performance:

◩ Identify the 'gaps' forecast in longer-term performance or strategy delivery, and which of them are likely to have their roots in the capabilities and characteristics of the organisation.

◩ Identify any shortfalls in short-term performance that have organisational roots.

Then, identify all important groups of *change actions* that will need to be taken to achieve the best 'fit' between the strategies, goals and performance of the enterprise and the design and capabilities of the organisation. Plan these organisational changes and define who is responsible for these actions and the follow-up process. Such actions should identify what can be done from within the organisation and what will require external intervention or support. This requires an objective assessment of the change management capabilities of the organisation.

Part Two – typical content

The content of Part 2 should be directly informed by the business and organisation review covered in Part 1.

Review and discussion of:

◩ the appropriateness and effectiveness of key teams and business functions

◩ key managers – performance, problems, potential and development needs

◩ identification of key people needs, currently and for the next period, and what will be done to meet them through recruitment and development

◘ definition of key development and training needs, and their links to business strategies

◘ the major HR processes, and the degree to which they contribute to the performance of the organisation; identification of needs for development, modification or enhancement

◘ definition of HR resourcing needs and what skills, manning and investment in major HR programmes will be needed to support the business.

Then, summarise all the *goals and actions* identified, and prioritise them. Make sure the agenda is deliverable and responsibilities are clearly identified for the next planning period. General managers should track the progress of this agenda, and its impact on the business.

The key output from the perspective of developing management capability is a clear view of the contribution expected from managers to today's and tomorrow's business models, and a business-centred brief for managers and developers to work from.

The following case examples show how differently organisations approach the integration of management development and business planning priorities:

Shell's systematic and integrated processes focus on business results.

1 **Talent review process**. This is an annual process that identifies the future talent requirements of each Shell Business and assesses the talent available to meet these demands through, for example, a ratio of identified candidates for every senior level position within the organisation.

2 **Strategy development**. Shell's annual strategy planning divides the entire business into some 50 Strategic Planning Units (SPUs). The strategy planning process uses (amongst other techniques) a traffic light system to highlight areas of strategic risk: for example, red would indicate an area requiring urgent attention. HR considerations are part of the strategy planning, although until recently, the main focus was on the skills required for new businesses, for example, project management. Shell is now integrating its talent review process with business planning so that 'every time we think about business improvement we think about the capabilities required of our managers'. The strength of this process is that it allows challenging dialogue about leadership and management capability.

3 **The concept of 'potential'**. This is an assessment of each individual in terms of the job level they could ultimately achieve in Shell, assuming unlimited job opportunity and full mobility. Historically it has been an assessment primarily of intellectual capability. In recent years there has been a shift to include a greater assessment of results delivery capability. For Shell, the strength in focusing on 'potential' is that it promotes a common language around management and leadership which is reflected in the current learning and development programmes.

Seizing opportunities to raise the quality of the dialogue about management capability at Consignia

Levers for raising the dialogue about management in Consignia have been

1 The board's interest in ensuring there is a clear line of sight from strategic direction to team and individual capabilities. Senior management in HR has proactively engaged the board in developing this 'line of sight'. Consignia's 'balanced scorecard' has helped to focus a dialogue on management capability to deliver business performance. And it is recognised that building the scorecard to review the requirements of management roles in the future is a priority and a key value-adding opportunity for the HR function.

2 The entry into new business ventures and partnerships in some parts of the business, which has focused attention on rigorous business planning, costs and individual management competency to deliver.

Engaging staff in strategic planning at the Civil Service College

The director of the Civil Service College is clear that the process of strategic planning within the college must itself be designed not only to foster the management capabilities that the civil service is seeking, but also to build widespread ownership of the results among staff as well. The process is perceived and managed as both an engagement process and a learning process, and hence a management/staff development process in itself. It has started outside the performance management framework.

To date the strategic management process has included:

- a hexagon process composed of 12 people from across the college; they worked in pairs – each exploring a strategic theme for the college which had been set by the college executive management team. One member of each pair examined the theme from an internal college perspective, the other considered it from a market and environmental view

- using the EFQM framework for assessing the state of management of the college

- a process of 'appreciative enquiry' which involves visioning, and engaging staff about the future of the organisation by drawing out the positive experiences and processes of the past.

Chapter 4 addresses key implementation issues:

◘ **managing the specification, design and delivery of management development**

◘ **evaluating investment in management development against business outcomes**

◘ **highlights emerging practice from case study organisations.**

4 | Managing learning: Getting the implementation right

Armed with the results of a business, organisation and management review (see previous chapter), development managers can begin to shape learning plans and initiatives. Managing development involves a series of processes, from diagnosis and specification, through implementation and evaluation. The key is to gear these processes to contribute to sustained business performance, and to remember that the way you organise and manage to deliver on Purpose 1 is different from Purpose 2 (see Table 1, page 10).

In practice, our study found that these processes are managed more or less well in organisations, leading to mixed results. You may want to consider your own priorities for improvement within your own business context. What follows is a review of the main findings from the survey that we carried out as part of this project.

Diagnosis

At the heart of diagnosis is a clear and purposeful description of the management capabilities required to deliver the current or future business models and to sustain or strengthen innovation. The quality of diagnosis is enhanced by the effective involvement of senior executives, learners

and those who have a stake in the outcome of any learning, such as customers. Business-centred people development specialists who have good relationships with line managers can play a key leadership role in this process. But this issue is too important to leave solely to HR.

Some of the greatest difficulties occur at this stage. While over 80 per cent of those who responded to our survey reported that line managers and senior executives are involved in diagnosis, only 13 per cent said this involvement was 'very effective'. Fewer than half of those who responded were involving those who were affected by the effectiveness with which learners play their roles, and only 7 per cent said they were 'very effective' at this. The majority of processes for diagnosis were only partly established and, at best, only partially effective.

Specification

This is fundamentally about designing management learning opportunities that are 'fit for purpose'. In complex dynamic environments, the development of managers must respond to significant work issues, clarify the context and produce valuable outputs. This means it is important to involve top management closely so that sensitive issues can be handled and proposals implemented. It also means that we need to see learning initiatives as part of business, organisational or HR activities, and not treat them as something separate. In order to specify management development, collaborative partner relationships with consultants/providers can be very valuable.

Surprisingly, 58 per cent of respondents rated their organisations as either 'effective' or 'very effective' in designing management education that is appropriate for its purpose. But, given the widespread issues about diagnosis and strategic management, we suspect that in most cases this purpose is unlikely to be a business purpose.

> *'The goal must be to be innovative enough in choice of methods to make a substantial difference to behaviour and performance...'*

Implementation

The key is to use learning processes that really do work. Our survey found that some of the more effective ones in delivering desired outcomes appear to be:

◘ project and action learning work (43 per cent)

◘ internal management courses (41 per cent)

◘ coaching (36 per cent).

Least effective processes were seen to be:

◘ simulations (3 per cent)

◘ distance learning and internet packages (3.2 per cent)

◘ visiting speakers and experts (8.1 per cent).

The biggest gaps between the use of methods and their perceived effectiveness for delivering desired outcomes were for external seminars and conferences, distance learning and Internet packages, visiting speakers and experts, and courses for a management qualification.

The goal must be to be innovative enough in choice of methods to make a substantial difference to behaviour and performance, even if these methods do not conform to conventional expectations. It is worth remembering that most learning in organisations is on-the-job or influenced by others, rather than from formal learning processes.

Over 50 per cent or respondents rated their organisations as effective in managing providers. Yet, curiously, the survey also revealed widespread and neglected needs for innovation: in responding to a diversity of learners, in ensuring learning retains its currency and in challenging people to create their own learning. Only 22 per cent were experimenting with the latest technology to deliver management education. This is surprising, considering the interest it has generated recently in the USA, and its obvious potential contribution for Purpose 1 learning.

Evaluation

The point of evaluation is to know whether you have made a difference and to learn from experience. This can be done on an individual, team or organisational level. If we are interested in sustained business performance then organisation-level assessment is particularly important. For example, if we set out to improve customer and employee satisfaction through leadership development than we should expect to measure these aspects of business performance both before the initiative and afterwards, on a time-frame that makes sense. These aspects of business performance can be given a financial value if we are seeking to do a business case or a cost-benefit analysis. We can also identify indicators, or measures, for changes in the effectiveness of management processes such as strategic planning.

> **'If we are interested in sustained business performance then organisation-level assessment is particularly important'**

Evaluation is a subject that aroused strong passions among those who participated in the research. One group felt that 'if you can't measure it, you can't manage it' and that the organisation had to find business measures of the added value of learning. Another group believed that the reason for investing in developing managers was obvious – 'If it walks like a duck, quacks like a duck, then it's a duck'. If we are serious about adding value to the business then we must be serious about evaluation of business outcomes. But we need to find pragmatic ways of achieving this that do not in themselves add significant cost to our operations.

Figure 1 | Evaluating the performance of management development

ORGANISATION FOCUSED

Changes in organisational performance specified at the time of planning	18%
Changes in the effectiveness of management processes	18%
Feedback from other stakeholders, eg customers	12%
Changes in the quality of the organisation's business plans	10%
Questionnaires completed by participants	78%
Feedback from line managers of particioants	65%
Discussions and group feedback by participants	47%
Analysis of changes in individual performance and career progress	41%
Feedback from providers	22%

INDIVIDUAL FOCUSED

Currently, evaluation is undertaken largely at the individual level, with a reliance on participant questionnaires and feedback. Figure 1 tells the story – organisation-focused evaluation is only a minority activity. This does not suggest a business-like approach to managing the development of managers. Without making an attempt to specify the intended benefits, and value some of the sizeable investments being made, they may be judged on cost grounds by default. In organisations that focus on current year earnings/costs it is particularly important to be explicit about the intended added value over a period of time, and to assess the actual contribution.

So how can it be done? There is evidence that thinking and practice on evaluation is evolving, so that the development of managers is becoming an integral part of the process of reviewing business development and organisational performance (see cases in Chapter 3).

Performance imperatives drive the evaluation of management development at Shell

Evaluating the contribution of leadership development to corporate performance has become an imperative in Shell.

Investing in management development has long been embedded in its cultural history. The drive for value creation across the businesses is requiring in-depth assessment of value to the business of this investment. Evaluation of the effectiveness of leadership development investment is likely to be through detailed senior management assessment rather than focusing only on more simplistic cost-benefit analysis.

Evaluating the contribution of management development to managing business risk will be a key feature at Consignia

'Increasing the velocity of change in management development to match the velocity of change in the business generally and to ensure the right delivery mechanisms for developing managers will be the key challenge' (Group HR director, Consignia).

This requires a different approach to assessing the value of management development, and places tighter emphasis on its contribution to business outcomes. Consignia is exploring new measures, for example the number of customer bids won first time round, and the quality of business proposals. The underlying principle is to assess whether risk to the business has reduced as a result of investing in managers.

Shifting from administrating management development to integrating it with the business requires:

◘ high-quality processes

◘ strong relationships between business and development leaders.

Consider the capability checklist as basis for action.

5 | Reviewing your organisation's capability for developing managers

The UK has some outstanding examples of organisations pursuing leading-edge strategies for developing managers for business success.

Our research findings also confirm that many organisations seem to have serious weaknesses in integrating management development into their business. Shifting from simply administering management development to integrating it with other business development activities depends on high-quality processes that support business linkages, and strong relationships between business and development leaders. Action in these areas needs to reflect the nature of your business and is both a corporate and business-level challenge. If you are keen to make progress on this challenge, then the checklist that follows will help you to take stock of where you think your business is today. You may wish to consider the checklist with colleagues as a way of engaging them in the challenge and developing a shared agenda for improvement and change.

A good practice checklist for capability developers

If you want to take further positive action to develop your organisation's management capability as a platform for sustained business performance, then start by considering these questions.

How would you rate your performance on the following?

Making the case for investing and developing managers

1   Convincing key stakeholders in your organisation of the significance of managers and leaders in organisational performance.

Significant improvement required	Some improvement required	No improvement required	Significant strength
☐	☐	☐	☐

2   Clarifying the business purpose of developing managers in your organisation.

Significant improvement required	Some improvement required	No improvement required	Significant strength
☐	☐	☐	☐

3   Identifying blockages that prevent you making headway in making the case.

Significant improvement required	Some improvement required	No improvement required	Significant strength
☐	☐	☐	☐

4   Breaking down blockages that prevent you making headway in making the case.

Significant improvement required	Some improvement required	No improvement required	Significant strength
☐	☐	☐	☐

Making the connection between business plans, organisation and management capabilities

5   Getting your organisation's plan to specify the management/ organisational capabilities needed to deliver it.

Significant improvement required	Some improvement required	No improvement required	Significant strength
☐	☐	☐	☐

6   Achieving the right balance between sustaining the current business model and developing future ones.

Significant improvement required	Some improvement required	No improvement required	Significant strength
☐	☐	☐	☐

7   Securing effective processes to sustain a fruitful organisational dialogue about developing managers and the organisation.

Significant improvement required	Some improvement required	No improvement required	Significant strength
☐	☐	☐	☐

Managing learning for business success

8 Ensuring the diagnostic process in your organisation clarifies the business requirements of managers with precision and is iterative.

Significant improvement required	Some improvement required	No improvement required	Significant strength
☐	☐	☐	☐

9 Ensuring the diagnostic process in your organisation is responsive to the changing business requirements of managers.

Significant improvement required	Some improvement required	No improvement required	Significant strength
☐	☐	☐	☐

10 Identifying where you need to be more ambitious or innovative in what you specify /design and how that is delivered.

Significant improvement required	Some improvement required	No improvement required	Significant strength
☐	☐	☐	☐

11 Creating evaluation processes that give you enough feedback on the actual benefits to the organisation that you need to achieve.

Significant improvement required	Some improvement required	No improvement required	Significant strength
☐	☐	☐	☐

12 Sustaining a consistent approach across business, organisational and development activities.

Significant improvement required	Some improvement required	No improvement required	Significant strength
☐	☐	☐	☐

Appendix 1 | About the research – scope, objectives, philosophy and methodology

The main aim of the research was to explore the contribution of management education and development to corporate performance; and in particular, the links between business strategy, organisation and management and the development of managers. The project builds on CIPD research exploring the relationship between people management practices and business performance and previous published material in this area. Key objectives were:

◘ to explore *current practice* and *capability* in identifying and managing the contribution of management development to corporate performance in the UK and Ireland

◘ to identify *good practice* in maximising the contribution of management education and development to corporate performance

◘ to develop a *practical framework*, in partnership with senior executives responsible for leading the development of managers, for connecting business strategies, organisation and management development requirements.

The relationship between management development and individual performance was beyond the scope of this project. Neither did it distinguish between leadership and management development. Rather, the project focused on the business outcomes of a range of education and development practices, in order to concentrate on meeting corporate performance challenges. Please use the vocabulary that reflects the language in your organisation.

The philosophy of the research

The philosophy of the research is grounded in the understanding that the quality of management is a key driver of sustained business performance and that since the role/contribution of management is highly organisation specific there is no 'one best way' for delivering business benefit from management development. Therefore, the 'approach' for linking management development to business performance challenges that was explored in this research recognises that executives make choices and decisions about the contribution of management development, and that these are contingent on, and contextual to, organisational circumstances.

The research was guided by an advisory group comprising senior executives from leading organisations in the public and private sectors, from management consultancies and representatives from government, and was carried out from June 2000 to December 2001.

Project Methodology

The quantitative study: A self-completion postal questionnaire was sent in June 2000 to 2900 randomly selected senior executive members of the Chartered Institute of Personnel and Development. Senior executives were defined as anyone who is accountable for the performance of an organisation that employs a substantial number of people. CIPD members who are senior executives are:

◘ a director or senior manager who works for an organisation employing 500 people or more *and* who earns £45,000+ per annum, or

◘ a director who works for an organisation employing 100 people or more *and* who earns £70,000+ per annum.

In total, 433 organisations responded, representing an overall response rate of 15 per cent. A profile of the respondents from the postal survey is shown in Table 2

Table 2 | Profile of respondents

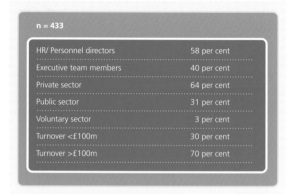

n = 433	
HR/ Personnel directors	58 per cent
Executive team members	40 per cent
Private sector	64 per cent
Public sector	31 per cent
Voluntary sector	3 per cent
Turnover <£100m	30 per cent
Turnover >£100m	70 per cent

The qualitative study:

◘ Seven consultation groups with personnel and development directors and senior general managers were held across the UK in the winter 2000, each lasting about two hours. The discussions followed a semi-structured schedule designed to gain insight into contrasting business and management development challenges and in particular the strategies and tactics used to address them.

◘ Twenty-five individual interviews were conducted in person with personnel / development directors and senior executives from leading organisations in the public and private sectors and business schools. The interviews were designed to explore in depth the process and relationship issues in linking business performance challenges with management development.

◘ A senior executive seminar was held in February 2001 to explore interim conclusions with a wider group of senior executives.

◘ Group discussions were held with senior executives in general management, personnel and management/leadership development in four organisations. The group discussions were designed to develop further the good practice framework in the realities of the business challenges facing particular organisations. The organisations were selected to reflect different sector/performance influences and levels and history of investment in management development.

Further background information on the case study organisations participating in the qualitative study can be found in Appendix 2.

Appendix 2 | Business context of and background to the case study organisations

Christ's Hospital Foundation

Christ's Hospital is a charitable foundation with a long history. Founded in the 16th century, its mission is to provide outstanding education and care to children whose families are in need. Its primary vehicle for realising this mission is currently a School also called Christ's Hospital, an institution with more than 800 boarding pupils that is located in a 200-acre site in rural Sussex.

Christ's Hospital is the UK's seventeenth largest charity by assets. Its funds derive from investment returns, donations, the activities of its commercial subsidiary (Christ's Hospital Enterprises) and from school fees paid by a minority of those who are enrolled in its School. Parents pay according to their means; as a result some 40 per cent of pupils are fully funded by the Foundation.

The Foundation is facing pressures for change on several fronts. The first set of pressures arise from its aspiration to raise the number of beneficiaries of its work. Second, there are pressures arising from the need to invest in premises and facilities, including IT, in order to underpin and sustain the outstanding quality of its charitable activities. A third set of pressures are coming from the need to respond to new regulatory regimes. Its School is being opened to the same kinds of scrutiny and legislative requirements as schools in the state sector, while the Foundation itself is facing government-led challenges to increase its performance and impact, its transparency and its accountability.

Effective response to these pressures requires not only more income and better management of resources; it also calls for a more entrepreneurial and commercial orientation and skills, better management information, and new ways of organising, managing and governing the work of the Foundation. All of these imperatives are profoundly affecting the roles of those who work for Christ's Hospital and its mission.

The Civil Service College

Founded 31 years ago, the business of the Civil Service College, now a directorate of Centre for Management and Policy Studies (CMPS) in the Cabinet Office, is to deliver learning opportunities to the UK public sector and to emerging democracies internationally. After a period of several years as an executive agency during the 1990s, the College was reintegrated into the core of the Cabinet Office as part of CMPS in the year 2000. It is now one of three business units within the CMPS of the Cabinet Office.

It currently employs about 280 permanent staff, of whom 80 are engaged in teaching. Programmes are also delivered by approximately 600 associates, who work through a variety of contractual arrangements. College staff work within a matrix structure. In 2001 the college served 32,000 learners, with turnover of over £21m. It is required to break even or generate a surplus to re-invest in the wider business.

At present about two-thirds of the of its work responds to the professional learning and development needs of individual public servants, who book themselves on to college programmes. The remaining third is commissioned by government departments and agencies, and largely focuses on facilitating organisational development. About 12 per cent of its work is consultancy to developing countries, and to the accession countries to the EU.

The overarching imperative for the college over the coming three to five years is to demonstrate to a variety of stakeholders that it can equip people who work in the public sector to make the difference that will deliver the current corporate aspirations of the UK government. In doing this, the college itself must mirror the goals and focus of the new Civil Service Public Service Delivery and Reform Agenda in its own business and management objectives. At the same time, it must continue to be an efficient business, in a marketplace where it must compete for customers and clients, and for financial and human resources.

The six main themes of the Civil Service reform:

- stronger leadership with a clear sense of purpose
- better business planning from top to bottom
- sharper performance management
- a dramatic improvement in diversity
- a service more open to people and ideas, which brings on talent
- a better deal for staff.

This strategic challenge marks a distinctive step change, not only from its early years as a centrally-funded body in a pre-competitive environment, but also from its time as an executive agency. As an agency, the primary goal had become its year-on-year financial performance (where, for example, the primary objective for staff had become the achievement of personal financial targets).

The college appointed a new director two and a half years ago. To him and his executive team it was apparent that the existing business model of the college, which had evolved to respond to its status as an agency, would no longer be sufficient for meeting the new imperatives that it now faced. The business model would need to be transformed, and this would require a strategic planning process.

Consignia

Consignia employs over 200,000 people across the business, of whom 140,000 are employed in Service Delivery, Royal Mail. Other recognised business brands within the Consignia Group include Parcelforce Worldwide and the Post Office. Consignia employs approximately 40,000 managers across the Group at all levels, from front-line upwards. It became a public limited company in 2001, but remains wholly owned by the government. Consignia is no longer the sole UK postal administrator, but a postal operator, licensed and regulated by Postcomm and subject to the rules of a regulated industry.

The business is organised into a series of market-facing, operating, and support units with a small group centre. The structure was put in place to achieve market focus, but does rely on a degree of matrix organisation to achieve overall Consigna goals.

Increased regulation and competition in the market is driving a number of performance imperatives at Consignia. These include the need for:

- greater customer focus
- greater commercial awareness and focus
- a step change in the cost structure
- new capabilities for responding to and absorbing change
- new capabilities to exploit related businesses, eg logistics
- stronger leadership with a clear sense of purpose.

Shell

The objectives of the RoyalDutch/Shell Group of Companies are to engage efficiently, responsibly and profitably in the oil, gas, chemicals and other selected businesses and participate in the research and development of other sources of energy. The Group directly employs 95,000 people worldwide and contributes to the economies of over 135 countries.

Shell's strategy is structured around the theme of: 'growing value through robust profitability and competitive edge'.
There is a focus not only on financial performance but on other drivers of performance and value creation, for example management capability.

The management development challenge facing Shell is to ensure an excellent supply of current and future talented managers to meet the needs of the business strategy. These managers must be capable of making the most of Shell's existing businesses and gaining new business, through expansion of current businesses and breaking new ground.

References and Bibliography

COURT S. (2001)

'Executive economics'. *People Management*. 26 July. p49.

DE GEUS A. (1999)

The Living Company: Growth, learning and longevity in business.
London, Nicolas Brealey Publishing.

DRUCKER P. F. (1999)

Management Challenges for the 21st Century. Oxford,
Butterworth-Heinemann.

MARKIDES C.C. (2000)

All The Right Moves: A guide to crafting breakthrough strategy.
Boston, Mass., Harvard Business School Press. p ix

SHAREHOLDER VALUE MAGAZINE (2000)

'The shareholder value 100'. *Shareholder Value Magazine*.
October-November. pp 16–27.

STAUNTON M. and GILES K. (2001)

'Age of enlightenment'. *People Management*. 26 July. pp 30–33.

TATE W. (2000)

Emergent Business Models. (unpublished.) Council for Excellence
in Management Leadership, October.

VALUEPARTNERSHIP LTD

www.valuepartnership.co.uk